Helpful Guide To Understanding "The Chosen" Season One

Dr. Rick Gillespie-Mobley

D1715150

DEDICATION

I dedicate this book to all the people I have been blessed to serve as their pastor at Roxbury Presbyterian Church, Glenville Presbyterian Church, Glenville New Life Community Church, New Life Fellowship, Calvary Presbyterian Church, and New Life At Calvary.

CONTENTS

ACKNOWLEDGMENTS

I am grateful to all those who made "The Chosen" possible for the body of Christ. Its inclusion of all races of people at the time of Jesus is exceptional. It's commitment to presenting the Scriptures in a a biblical fashion is a blessing to all who watch it. My goal is to help those with little biblical background knowledge to understand how the Scriptures are woven into the episodes. I truly believe you should watch an episode at least twice to discover the richness hidden inside each of them. I also want people to understand where the series include information not found in Scripture so that people will not go looking for things in the Bible that are not there.

INTRODUCTION

One of the purposes of "The Chosen" is to create characters with depth of life so that you can read the scriptures and understand why biblical characters may behave in the way that they do. "The Chosen" is not a biblical story as revealed in the Scriptures, but it is a story which contains the Scriptures and provides us with a possibility of how things may have taken place. If you accept it for what it is, you will be strengthened and encouraged in your faith. If you demand it be a literal rendition of the Scriptures, you will be disappointed in your search. "The Chosen" is a wonderful way to capture the heart, the emotions, and the essence of the characters in the Scriptures.

The purpose of this book is to help you understand how the Scriptures are woven into the story and to learn from both the lives of the characters and the teachings of Scripture. By providing you with a summary of the main characters in each episode, a summary of the content of the episode, and the Scriptures referred to in in the episode, you will be able to glean a greater understanding of what is happening as you watch.

There are questions for discussion that you can

use in a small group if you choose to use "The Chosen" as a bible study topic. The questions do not require a scholarly background to lead the discussion. The questions are a combination of your reactions to the characters and your application of the Scriptures. The number of questions you will use will depend on the size of your group and whether or not you have watched the episodes prior to meeting or not. Obviously, you will have more time for discussion if you watch the episodes prior to coming together.

"The Chosen" episodes are available for purchase on Amazon.com on dvd. The episodes can be watched for free on the on the Chosen website https://watch.thechosen.tv/. The episodes are also available for free on the Angel Studios App for phones and on the Angel Studio website at https://www.angel.com/watch/the-chosen.

Actual Biblical Characters Appearing In The Chosen Season 1

Andrew

40 Andrew, Simon Peter's brother, was one of the two who heard what John had said and who had followed Jesus. 41 The first thing Andrew did was to find his brother Simon and tell him, "We have found the Messiah" (that is, the Christ). 42 And he brought him to Jesus. *The New International Version* (Grand Rapids, MI: Zondervan, 2011), Jn 1:40–42.

Jacob

5 So he came to a town in Samaria called Sychar, near the plot of ground Jacob had given to his son Joseph. 6 Jacob's well was there, and Jesus, tired as he was from the journey, sat down by the well. It was about noon. *The New International Version* (Grand Rapids, MI: Zondervan, 2011), Jn 4:5–6.

James son of Alphaeus (Little James)

2 These are the names of the twelve apostles: first, Simon (who is called Peter) and his brother Andrew; James son of Zebedee, and his brother John; 3 Philip and Bartholomew; Thomas and Matthew the tax collector; James son of Alphaeus, and Thaddaeus; 4 Simon the Zealot and Judas Iscariot, who betrayed him.

James son of Zebedee (Big James)
21 Going on from there, he saw two other brothers, James son of Zebedee and his brother John. They were in a boat with their father Zebedee, preparing their nets. Jesus called them, 22 and immediately they left the boat and their father and followed him. *The New International Version* (Grand Rapids, MI: Zondervan, 2011), Mt 4:21–22.

Jesus As Twelve Year Old
41 Every year Jesus' parents went to Jerusalem for the Festival of the Passover. 42 When he was twelve years old, they went up to the festival, according to the custom. 43 After the festival was over, while his parents were returning home, the boy Jesus stayed behind in Jerusalem, but they were unaware of it

Jesus
35 The next day John was there again with two of his disciples. 36 When he saw Jesus passing by, he said, "Look, the Lamb of God!" 37 When the two disciples heard him say this, they followed Jesus. *The New International Version* (Grand Rapids, MI: Zondervan, 2011), Jn 1:35–37.

John
21 Going on from there, he saw two other brothers, James son of Zebedee and his brother John. They were in a boat with their father Zebedee, preparing their nets. Jesus called them, 22 and immediately they left the boat and their father and followed him. *The New*

International Version (Grand Rapids, MI: Zondervan, 2011), Mt 4:21–22.

John The Baptist
In those days John the Baptist came, preaching in the wilderness of Judea 2 and saying, "Repent, for the kingdom of heaven has come near." 3 This is he who was spoken of through the prophet Isaiah: "A voice of one calling in the wilderness, 'Prepare the way for the Lord, make straight paths for him.' " *The New International Version* (Grand Rapids, MI: Zondervan, 2011), Mt 3:1–3.

Joseph
48 When his parents saw him, they were astonished. His mother said to him, "Son, why have you treated us like this? Your father and I have been anxiously searching for you." *The New International Version* (Grand Rapids, MI: Zondervan, 2011), Lk 2:48.

Joshua
13 Then Moses set out with Joshua his aide, and Moses went up on the mountain of God *The New International Version* (Grand Rapids, MI: Zondervan, 2011), Ex 24:13.

Mary
48 When his parents saw him, they were astonished. His mother said to him, "Son, why have you treated us like this? Your father and I have been anxiously searching for you." *The New International Version* (Grand Rapids, MI: Zondervan, 2011), Lk 2:48.

Mary Magdalene

After this, Jesus traveled about from one town and village to another, proclaiming the good news of the kingdom of God. The Twelve were with him, 2 and also some women who had been cured of evil spirits and diseases: Mary (called Magdalene) from whom seven demons had come out; 3 Joanna the wife of Chuza, the manager of Herod's household; Susanna; and many others. These women were helping to support them out of their own means. *The New International Version* (Grand Rapids, MI: Zondervan, 2011), Lk 8:1–3.

Matthew

10 While Jesus was having dinner at Matthew's house, many tax collectors and sinners came and ate with him and his disciples. 11 When the Pharisees saw this, they asked his disciples, "Why does your teacher eat with tax collectors and sinners?" *The New International Version* (Grand Rapids, MI: Zondervan, 2011), Mt 9:10–11.

Moses

" So Moses prayed for the people. 8 The Lord said to Moses, "Make a snake and put it up on a pole; anyone who is bitten can look at it and live." 9 So Moses made a bronze snake and put it up on a pole. Then when anyone was bitten by a snake and looked at the bronze snake, they lived.

Nicodemus

"Now there was a Pharisee, a man named Nicodemus who was a member of the Jewish ruling council. 2 He came to Jesus at night and said, "Rabbi, we know that you are a teacher who has come from God. For no one could perform the signs you are doing if God were not with him."" *The New International Version* (Grand Rapids, MI: Zondervan, 2011), Jn 3:1–2.

38 Later, Joseph of Arimathea asked Pilate for the body of Jesus. Now Joseph was a disciple of Jesus, but secretly because he feared the Jewish leaders. With Pilate's permission, he came and took the body away. 39 He was accompanied by Nicodemus, the man who earlier had visited Jesus at night. Nicodemus brought a mixture of myrrh and aloes, about seventy-five pounds. 40 Taking Jesus' body, the two of them wrapped it, with the spices, in strips of linen. This was in accordance with Jewish burial customs *The New International Version* (Grand Rapids, MI: Zondervan, 2011), Jn 19:38–40.

Simon

40 Andrew, Simon Peter's brother, was one of the two who heard what John had said and who had followed Jesus. 41 The first thing Andrew did was to find his brother Simon and tell him, "We have found the Messiah" (that is, the Christ). 42 And he brought him to Jesus. *The New International Version* (Grand Rapids, MI: Zondervan, 2011), Jn 1:40–42.

Simon's Wife (Eden)

14 When Jesus came into Peter's house, he saw Peter's mother-in-law lying in bed with a fever. 15 He touched her hand and the fever left her, and she got up and began to

wait on him. *The New International Version* (Grand Rapids, MI: Zondervan, 2011), Mt 8:14–15.

5 Don't we have the right to take a believing wife along with us, as do the other apostles and the Lord's brothers and Cephas?*The New International Version* (Grand Rapids, MI: Zondervan, 2011), 1 Co 9:5.

Thaddaeus
2 These are the names of the twelve apostles: first, Simon (who is called Peter) and his brother Andrew; James son of Zebedee, and his brother John; 3 Philip and Bartholomew; Thomas and Matthew the tax collector; James son of Alphaeus, and Thaddaeus; 4 Simon the Zealot and Judas Iscariot, who betrayed him.

The Man With Leprosy
2 A man with leprosy came and knelt before him and said, "Lord, if you are willing, you can make me clean." *The New International Version* (Grand Rapids, MI: Zondervan, 2011), Mt 8:1–2.

The Men Bringing In The Paralyzed Man and The Paralyzed Man
Some men came, bringing to him a paralyzed man, carried by four of them. 4 Since they could not get him to Jesus because of the crowd, they made an opening in the roof above Jesus by digging through it and then lowered the mat the man was lying on. *The New International Version* (Grand Rapids, MI: Zondervan, 2011), Mk 2:3–4.

The Woman At The Well

28 Then, leaving her water jar, the woman went back to the town and said to the people, 29 "Come, see a man who told me everything I ever did. Could this be the Messiah?" 30 They came out of the town and made their way toward him. *The New International Version* (Grand Rapids, MI: Zondervan, 2011), Jn 4:28–30.

Thomas

24 Now Thomas (also known as Didymus), one of the Twelve, was not with the disciples when Jesus came. 25 So the other disciples told him, "We have seen the Lord!" But he said to them, "Unless I see the nail marks in his hands and put my finger where the nails were, and put my hand into his side, I will not believe." *The New International Version* (Grand Rapids, MI: Zondervan, 2011), Jn 20:24–25.

Zebedee

19 When he had gone a little farther, he saw James son of Zebedee and his brother John in a boat, preparing their nets. 20 Without delay he called them, and they left their father Zebedee in the boat with the hired men and followed him.

1 RESOURCES FOR EPISODE 1 I HAVE CALLED YOU BY NAME

Season 1 Episode 1 "I Have Called You By Name"
55 Minutes Viewing Time

The Main Characters:

Lillith—(Mary Magdalene)—The person who is demon possessed.

Nicodemus—The Pharisee from Jerusalem visiting Capernaum.

Quintus Dominus—Roman Magistrate who wants to catch Jewish fisherman who are not paying taxes on the fish they catch on the Sabbath (Shabbath).

Matthew—The tax collector who is very wealthy, but despised. He gives Andrew and Simon a very hard time with their taxes.

Gaius—The Roman soldier who guards Matthew while he is collecting taxes.

Rabbi Shmuel—Young Pharisee in charge of the synagogue in Capernaum and is a strict interpreter of the Law.

Simon and Andrew—Two brothers who are unable to pay their taxes. They attempt to fix a fight at Simon's urging in order to cover their debt.

Simon's wife (Eden)—The young woman who encourages Simon to go to synagogue.

Jesus—The unexpected guest that appears in the tavern and does something extraordinary.

Summary of Episode 1 I Have Called You By Name

The episode begins with Mary Magdalene as a little girl with her father. Her father appears to be ill. She wakes up in the middle of the night afraid but not quite sure why. He reminds her of Isaiah 43:1 so that she will not be afraid. The scene shifts to many years later in which she is now an adult and possessed by demons. There is an assumption that she is involved in prostitution. She attacks one of her clients by drawing blood from his neck with her nails. He runs for help, reporting that she is demon possessed.

Nicodemus is on his way to Capernaum but is

intercepted by the Roman magistrate Quintus. The magistrate wants Nicodemus's help in putting an end to Jews fishing on the Sabbath, because the fishermen were not paying taxes on their catches. Nicodemus speaks against the fishermen and the people eating fish on the Sabbath, but only because the fishermen are violating the Sabbath. Nicodemus will find himself called upon to cast the demons out of Mary who goes by the name Lillith. Everyone thinks her name is Lillith, because that's the name she has had since the demons possessed her.

Matthew is shown in his wealth as a tax collector. He attempts to get to his tax collector booth by paying a driver to take him to work under a blanket in a cart. Once at work, he has a Roman guard, Gaius, who is his protector. Matthew shows little sympathy or compassion for those unable to pay their taxes. He has no problem with late fees, compounded interest on late payments and the like.

Simon and Andrew are brothers who are behind in their taxes. They attempt to win money by fixing a fight between Simon and his brother-in law and betting on the fight. Simon has no problem trying to fish on the Sabbath to get some money to pay his taxes. He tries to hide his activity from his wife, Eden. Desperate, Simon finds himself making a deal with the Roman magistrate, Quintus, to turn in those Jewish fishermen who are fishing on the Sabbath to avoid paying taxes on their catch.

Lillith finds herself in a gambling bar full of all kinds of sin. The bartender tries to help her out. He appears to be her only friend. She gives him the one material possession she values most, before heading out to commit suicide. A dove intervenes before she jumps off a cliff and leads her back to the bar. She then encounters Jesus whom she rejects. When Jesus calls out "Mary Magdalene", it touches her heart .Jesus repeats Isaiah 41:1 to her. The demons are cast out.

Scriptures Woven Into Episode 1 I Have Called You By Name

But now, this is what the Lord says— he who created you, Jacob, he who formed you, Israel: "Do not fear, for I have redeemed you; I have summoned you by name; you are mine. 2 When you pass through the waters, I will be with you; and when you pass through the rivers, they will not sweep over you. When you walk through the fire, you will not be burned; the flames will not set you ablaze. *The New International Version* (Grand Rapids, MI: Zondervan, 2011), Is 43:1–2.

After this, Jesus traveled about from one town and village to another, proclaiming the good news of the kingdom of God. The Twelve were with him, 2 and also some women who had been cured of evil spirits and diseases: Mary (called Magdalene) from whom seven demons had come out; 3 Joanna the wife of Chuza, the manager of Herod's household; Susanna; and many others. These women were helping to support them out of their own means. *The New International Version* (Grand Rapids, MI: Zondervan, 2011), Lk 8:1–3.

Biblical Characters Who Are A Part Of Episode1 I Have Called You By Name

Mary Magdalene (Lillith)

The Scriptures do record Mary Magdalene as having been possessed by demons. Jesus does set her free by casting the demons out of her. The Scriptures do not record the interactions in the episode that she has with Nicodemus or any of the other characters. The name Lillith is given to her by the author to designate her name after the demons entered her.

Matthew The Tax Collector

The Scriptures do record Matthew as a tax collector. The Scriptures do not record any of Matthew's life prior to his meeting Jesus. The author is providing insight on the possible life of a tax collector during the time of Jesus.

Nicodemus The Pharisee

The Scriptures do record Nicodemus in the early and late stages of Jesus' ministry. The scenes involving Nicodemus are prior to his encounter with Jesus and are not found in Scriptures. The author is providing insight to the way the Jewish Councils carried out their duties and how the Pharisees related to each other.

Andrew & Simon

The Scriptures do record Andrew and Simon as being brothers and fishermen. The Scriptures do not record them being behind in their taxes or plotting with the Romans to catch fishermen who were evading taxes on their catch.

Simon's Wife (Eden)

Although the Scriptures indicate Peter was married, his wife's name is never mentioned. Eden is the name assigned to her by the authors of the Chosen. The

Scriptures do no record any of the conversations of Simon with his wife. The author is adding character to depth to Simon and his wife.

Jesus
The Scriptures do record Jesus casting out demons from Mary Magdalene but they do not record him meeting her in this particular setting of a tavern.

Bible Study Discussion Questions For Episode 1
"I Have Called You By Name"

1. At the beginning of the show as it was coming on, what was the significance of the fish turning blue and changing directions?

2. Why did Nicodemus agree to appear to help the Romans by condemning the Jewish fishermen who were making a catch of fish on the Sabbath?

3. Why does Matthew have to take all the precautions that he does just to make it to work?

4. Have you ever been tempted to look down on someone because of the kind of work they do? What if their work was illegal?

5. Were you surprised by the number of different races portrayed in Episode 1, for instance Matthew being asked for help from a Black man or Nicodemus talking with a Black woman? When you read the Scriptures, do you tend to see multiple races in your mind or just one?

6. What do you think troubled Nicodemus the most after his encounter with Lillith, his reputation or his doubts about his understanding of God?

7. What kind of character does Simon appear to be to you?

8. What do you think Matthew is thinking as he sits and collects taxes from people who obviously seem poor? Does he seem happy to you?

9. Simon agrees to turn in Jews fishing on the Sabbath. How is his betrayal of his people different from Matthew's role as a tax collector?

10. What drives Mary to the point of wanting to take her life? How do you interpret the bird that appears just as she was about to jump off the cliff?

11. Has there ever been a "bird moment" in your life that kept you from making a bad choice? What form did your bird take?

12. Why do you think the first appearance of Jesus in "The Chosen" has him in a place where all kind of negative behavior is taking place with drunkenness, gambling, and soliciting for prostitution?

13. What does Jesus do that turns the corner completely for Mary from rejection to acceptance?

14. What did Jesus do to get your attention to cause you to turn toward him?

15. Why was Jesus' final quotation of Isaiah 43:1 to Mary so powerful when he quoted it to her?

16. What feeling did you have inside as you watched Jesus lay his hands on Mary's head and heal her as she cried?

17. What would you like to see Jesus cast out of your life, so that you can grow in Christ?

2 RESOURCES FOR EPISODE 2 SHABBAT

Episode 2 Shabbat
39 Minutes Viewing Time

The Main Characters:

Mary Magdalene—the woman who has had demons cast out of her by Jesus.

Nicodemus—Pharisee who wants to question Mary to find out how her healing took place.

Matthew—The tax collector who wants to share his feelings that Simon is not a trustworthy individual and perhaps Quintus has made a mistake waiving his taxes. He is determined to collect all taxes due to Rome.

Gaius—The Roman soldier who attempts to persuade Matthew to give up the foolish notion of going to see Quintus.

Quintus Dominus—Roman Magistrate who threatens to

kill Matthew and Gaius the centurion for disturbing him. Quintus is impressed with Matthew.

Rabbi Joseph—Young Pharisee who reports to others that he has seen Mary healed and in her right mind.

Simon and Andrew—Two brothers who have a scheme to turn in other Jews who are fishing on the Sabbath to avoid paying taxes to the Romans. The brothers are at odds over the agreement with Quintus.

Simon's wife (Eden)—She can sense that her husband Simon is up to something that is probably not good.

Summary Of Episode 2 Shabbat

The story begins in the year 948 BC with an explanation of why the Sabbath (Shabbat) is important as a day of rest. A mother explains to her son that Shabbat is a chance to honor their family, their people and their God. After a blessing is given to a boy and a girl, a man begins to recite from Proverbs about a virtuous woman. They then begin to share in the Shabbat meal together.

The story then shifts to Mary Magdalene a few days after she had been healed by Jesus. She is with other women in a hair salon, and is encouraged to use her skill in braiding hair. Mary attempts the process. But Mary's heart is on preparing to host her first Shabbat meal.

While in the marketplace, Mary is spotted by one of the Pharisees who accompanied Nicodemus when he tried to cast the demons out of her. The Pharisee informs the other religious leaders of Mary's healing, believing that Nicodemus had been successful in casting the demons out of her. The Pharisees hold a meeting to discuss the miracle that has taken place. Nicodemus insists on finding Mary and discovering what had actually happened to her. Her response leaves him with more questions than answers.

Against the Roman soldier Gaius's advice, Matthew insists on going to speak to the Roman leader, Dominus, to confirm Simon's story about Simon's and his brother's taxes having been paid in full. Gaius believes it is a suicide mission to disturb Dominus, let alone question him. Matthew demonstrates a boldness that nearly costs him his life.

Simon continues his scheme to try to gather information from the merchants to discover who is fishing on the Sabbath and evading taxes. He buys drinks for them at the tavern in the hopes of getting them to talk more freely. His brother, Andrew, is upset with him over his bargain with Dominus and the Romans. Andrew can't get past it being a traitorous act. James and John are briefly introduced into the story.

The heart of the episode revolves around the preparations for the Shabbat meals that will take place later that day. Nicodemus and his wife are hosting a meal for all the important people in the community. Simon, his wife Eden, and Andrew are to share their meal together. Mary prepares her first Shabbat meal with a blind woman, a disabled man, two uninvited men, Thaddeus and James, who were told they would be welcome at her house, and a completely unexpected surprise guest. Matthew has his Shabbat meal with the most unusual guest of all. There is tension of some sort at each of the Shabbat meals.

Scriptures Woven Into Episode 2

Shabbat

"Remember the Sabbath day by keeping it holy. 9 Six days you shall labor and do all your work, 10 but the seventh day is a sabbath to the Lord your God. On it you shall not do any work, neither you, nor your son or daughter, nor your male or female servant, nor your animals, nor any foreigner residing in your towns. 11 For in six days the Lord made the heavens and the earth, the sea, and all that is in them, but he rested on the seventh day. Therefore the Lord blessed the Sabbath day and made it holy. *The New International Version* (Grand Rapids, MI: Zondervan, 2011), Ex 20:8–11.

A wife of noble character who can find? She is worth far more than rubies. 11 Her husband has full confidence in her and lacks nothing of value. 12 She brings him good, not harm, all the days of her life. 13 She selects wool and flax and works with eager hands. 14 She is like the merchant ships, bringing her food from afar. 15 She gets up while it is still night; she provides food for her family and portions for her female servants. 16 She considers a field and buys it; out of her earnings she plants a vineyard. 17 She sets about her work vigorously; her arms are strong for her tasks. 18 She sees that her trading is profitable, and her lamp does not go out at night. *The New International Version* (Grand Rapids, MI: Zondervan, 2011), Pr 31:10–18.

46 "Nazareth! Can anything good come from there?" Nathanael asked. "Come and see," said Philip. *The New International Version* (Grand Rapids, MI: Zondervan,

2011), Jn 1:46.

Biblical Characters Who Are Part Of Episode 2
Shabbat

Mary Magdalene
The Scriptures does record Jesus casting demons out of her. Even though much of this episode revolves arounds Mary's healing, the Scriptures do not record these additional events. None of the scenes involving the Shabbat meal are recorded in the Scriptures.

Matthew The Tax Collector
Mathew is recorded in the Scriptures, but the scenes in this episode are not recorded in the Scriptures. The author is attempting to show what the life of a tax collector may have been like.

Nicodemus The Pharisee
Nicodemus is actually found in the Scriptures, but the events in this episode surrounding his life are not recorded in the Scriptures. The author is attempting to show what the life of a Pharisee may have been like during this time period.

Andrew & Simon
The Scriptures do record Andrew and Simon as brothers. The Scriptures do not record the story of working with the Romans to catch fishermen who were fishing on the Sabbath to avoid paying taxes on their catch. The author is attempting to show the kinds of pressure people could fall under from the burden of Roman taxation.

Simon's Wife (Eden)
Although the Scriptures indicate Simon was married, his wife's name is never mentioned. Eden is the name assigned to her by the authors of the Chosen. The Scriptures do not record the interactions between Simon and his wife. The author is adding depth to the characters involved in the Chosen.

James & John
The Scriptures do record James and John as brothers, Jewish, and fishermen. They are only briefly introduced in this episode. This introduction is not recorded in the Scriptures. The author is attempting to help us understand Jewish culture from several different walks of life.

James & Thaddaeus
The Scriptures do record James and Thaddaeus as becoming disciples of Jesus, but there is nothing to indicate they shared the Shabbat meal with Mary and her guests along with Jesus.

Jesus
The Scriptures do record Jesus in several situations however, there is not a record of Jesus attending a Shabbat meal. By including him in the meal at Mary's home, the author, shows the humility of Jesus in a unique way.

Bible Study Discussion Question Episode 2 Shabbat

1. Why do you think God gave us the Sabbath, and why do you think we resist it so strongly?

2. What difference did you notice in Mary from the end of the first episode until the end of episode 2?

3. If you are a believer, what was the most significant change you noticed about yourself after giving your life to Christ?

4. Why is Gaius so bent on persuading Matthew to forget about talking to Quintus, and why is Matthew so determined to do it?

5. Do you notice anything unusual about Matthew in the way he relates to people?

6. Why is there such tension going on between Simon and Andrew at the tavern?

7. When have you and a close relative or a friend seen the same situation from totally opposite

perspectives? How did you maintain your relationship?

8. If you were giving advice to Simon on his plan with Quintus, what would you say to him?

9. Why does Nicodemus want to get to the bottom of what happened to Mary?

10. How do you relate to Mary's statement "I was one way, and now I am completely different, and that thing that happened in between was Him?"

11. Why do you think Simon isn't straightforward with his wife Eden about what he's really involved in?

12. What keeps us from being honest with others about what we are truly doing?

13. What feelings do you have for Matthew knowing he has been beaten up and watching him leave the house he desperately wanted to enter for the Shabbat meal?

14. What do you make of Nicodemus' statement "Who is responsible for repressing our worship? I think I know."

15. What contrasts do you see in the four Shabbat meals with one being in Simon's home, one in Mary's home, one in Nicodemus' home and one being in Matthew's courtyard?

16. Which meal do you identify with the most in your current walk with the Lord?

17. What can we learn from Jesus in his declining to lead the Shabbat meal?

3 RESOURCES FOR EPISODE 3 JESUS LOVES THE LITTLE CHILDREN

Episode 3 Jesus Loves The Little Children
30 Minutes Viewing Time
The Main Characters:

Jesus—He is preparing to begin his public ministry and is the teacher of children.

Abigail—She is a little girl who stumbles into Jesus' home in the fields and senses that Jesus is a good man. She's very knowledgeable with the Scriptures.

Joshua The Brave—He is the first person Abigail brings back with her to meet Jesus.

Boys & Girls—They ask Jesus questions, that provide insight into the ministry that lies ahead for Jesus.

Summary of Episode 3 Jesus Loves The Little Children

The episode begins with Jesus living in a field outside of Capernaum. He has His own personal campsite set up where He prays, sleeps, works, and cooks. Jesus has two requests in that He wants God to glorify Him with Himself, and He wants the Father to speak through him. From the things that Jesus has carved out as a carpenter, you can see a transition is taking place. Jesus is preparing to make himself known to others. He has not yet begun his ministry and at present He has not called any of the disciples.

While Jesus is living in the field, a little girl stumbles across his camp. She sees him, but runs away. Her name is Abigail. The next day she brings her friend, Joshua, to meet Jesus. Jesus gives him the name Joshua the Brave. The next day, the two of them bring additional friends to meet Jesus. They ask Jesus if they can hang around for a while, and Jesus assigns them all a task while they are there with him.

The children have several questions that they ask of Jesus, and Jesus has questions for them. Through their dialoguing, Jesus begins to reveal His mission and starts teaching them some of the things He will later teach to His disciples. This episode is not found anywhere in the Scriptures and there is no record of Jesus spending time with this age group in the Bible. However, the episode is loaded with Scriptural references to indicate what Jesus would do in the near future. Jesus begins to plant seeds that the Messiah is not going to be a military conqueror, who will overthrow the Roman government. The episode ends with Jesus leaving behind a gift with a personal touch for Abigail.

Scriptures Woven Into Episode Three
Jesus Loves The Little Children

"Where did this man get these things?" they asked. "What's this wisdom that has been given him? What are these remarkable miracles he is performing? 3 Isn't this the carpenter? Isn't this Mary's son and the brother of James, Joseph, Judas and Simon? Aren't his sisters here with us?" And they took offense at him. *The New International Version* (Grand Rapids, MI: Zondervan, 2011), Mk 6:2–3.

4 Hear, O Israel: The Lord our God, the Lord is one. 5 Love the Lord your God with all your heart and with all your soul and with all your strength. 6 These commandments that I give you today are to be on your hearts. 7 Impress them on your children. Talk about them when you sit at home and when you walk along the road, when you lie down and when you get up. 8 Tie them as symbols on your hands and bind them on your foreheads. 9 Write them on the doorframes of your houses and on your gates. *The New International Version* (Grand Rapids, MI: Zondervan, 2011), Dt 6:4–9.

1 How good and pleasant it is when God's people live together in unity! *The New International Version* (Grand Rapids, MI: Zondervan, 2011), Ps 133:1.

18 " 'Do not seek revenge or bear a grudge against anyone among your people, but love your neighbor as yourself. I am the Lord. "*The New International Version* (Grand Rapids, MI: Zondervan, 2011), Le 19:18.

"Why do you listen when men say, 'David is bent on harming you'? 10 This day you have seen with your own eyes how the Lord delivered you into my hands in the cave. Some urged me to kill you, but I spared you; I said, 'I will not lay my hand on my lord, because he is the Lord's anointed. *The New International Version* (Grand Rapids, MI: Zondervan, 2011), 1 Sa 24:9–10.

The Spirit of the Sovereign Lord is on me, because the Lord has anointed me to proclaim good news to the poor. He has sent me to bind up the brokenhearted, to proclaim freedom for the captives and release from darkness for the prisoners, 2 to proclaim the year of the Lord's favor
The New International Version (Grand Rapids, MI: Zondervan, 2011), Is 61:1–2.

9 "This, then, is how you should pray:" 'Our Father in heaven, hallowed be your name, 10 your kingdom come, your will be done, on earth as it is in heaven. 11 Give us today our daily bread. 12 And forgive us our debts, as we also have forgiven our debtors. 13 And lead us not into temptation, but deliver us from the evil one.' *The New International Version* (Grand Rapids, MI: Zondervan, 2011), Mt 6:9–13.

Biblical Characters Who Are Part Of Episode 3-
Jesus Loves The Little Children

Jesus

The Scriptures do record that Jesus called a little child to him and that he told the disciples to not hinder the children from coming to him. The Scriptures do record that Jesus was a carpenter. However, the Scriptures do not record the events that take place in this episode.

Bible Study Discussion Questions Episode 3
Jesus Loves The Little Children

1. Prior to viewing this episode, did you ever think of Jesus traveling alone, living in the wild, doing just enough carpentry work to get by in life? If not, what was your view of Jesus as a carpenter prior to him starting his ministry?

2. What significance if any do you attach to the little boat that Jesus had carved out that was sitting on the bench?

3. Why is Jesus praying that the Father would speak through Him?

4. Why does the author show us Jesus starting a fire from kindling, Jesus cooking, and Jesus washing his feet?

5. Why do you think Abigail was attracted to Jesus? What qualities do you see in her?

6. How does Jesus use humor to reach Abigail and Joshua The Brave? How can we use humor to reach people today?

7. What do you notice about the way Jesus interacted with the children?

8. Do you view kids with as much spiritual capacity as Jesus did? Why or Why not?

9. Why do you think Jesus said that his favorite food was "bread?"

10. When you use your imagination to visualize Jesus with children in the bible, are the children in your mind as racially diverse as were those in this episode? How is the diversity among the children, helpful to our understanding of the body of Christ and of God?

11. What is Jesus saying to us when he told the youth, "Everyone has a larger job than just their trade?"

12. Who do the youth say that Jesus is and what is their basis for the claims that they make?

13. Who are people saying that Jesus is today, and what are their claims based upon?

14. What did you think of Jesus injuring his hand and having to put a bandage on his wrist after burning himself? Why didn't he just heal the spot?

15. What do you think was the purpose of Jesus leaving behind the special gift of two carved horses for Abigail?

16. If Jesus were to leave behind a special gift for you today, what would you like for it to be?

4 RESOURCES FOR EPISODE 4 THE ROCK ON WHICH IT IS BUILT

Episode 4 The Rock On Which It Is Built
49 Minutes Viewing Time

The Main Characters:

Simon—the fisherman who leads the Romans out onto the Sea of Galilee to catch Jews who are fishing on the Sabbath to evade taxes.

Andrew—Simon's brother who opposes Simon's plan with Quintus to betray the Jewish fishermen and is the one who discovers that Jesus is the Messiah.

Quintus—the Roman magistrate who hires Matthew to spy on Simon to make sure that Simon is not double crossing him on the agreement to turn in rogue Jewish fishermen.

Matthew—the tax collector who is eager to put his skills to work for Quintus in order to turn in Simon for tax evasion.

Eden—Simon's wife who challenges Simon on his faith in God and insists that she be allowed to take care of her ailing mother.

James & John—brothers who are fishermen who work for their father Zebedee.

Zebedee—a successful fisherman who has been catching fish on the Sabbath and is the father of James and John. He has several fishing boats.

Nicodemus—a Pharisee who is informed of the ministry of John the Baptist and insists on visiting John in prison.

John The Baptist—a preacher on the Jordan River insisting that people repent and be baptized for the forgiveness of their sins.

Summary Of Episode 4 Rock On Which It Is Built

The episode begins with Simon in a boat with Roman soldiers out on the Sea of Galilee searching for Jewish fishermen who are fishing on the Sabbath to avoid paying taxes on their catch. All is going well until Simon spots a fishing bobber. Attached to the bobber is an insignia that Peter recognizes, and it indicates the people they are after are very close friends of his. Simon has to come up with a strategy to keep the Romans from catching his friends who are currently also on the lake fishing. He puts his plan into action and it works.

The Roman commander on the ship believes that

Simon has not been fully honest with them, and as a warning, he cuts off a piece of Simon's ear. Simon decides to come clean with the friends he kept from having arrested and imprisoned hoping they would sympathize with him. They view him as a miserable traitor. All Simon wants in return, for keeping them out of jail, was for them to give him their catch of fish from that night. Things do not go as well as Simon had hoped.

Quintus begins to have second thoughts trusting Simon. He assigns Matthew the task of following Simon wherever he goes and to write down everything he notices about Simon. Matthew does his job diligently to the point of trying to get Simon to just give himself up to the Romans, because Simon had no possibility of paying off his debt. Simon insists on trying to the very end.

Rabbi Joseph, one of the Pharisees, comes and informs Nicodemus that John the Baptist has been arrested by the Romans. Nicodemus insists on finding John in prison so that he can have John answer some of his questions. This imprisonment is not found in the bible and is not to be confused with Herod's later arrest of John The Baptist.

When Simon goes home, he finds his two brothers-in-laws discussing an issue with his wife Eden. Their mother is very ill and someone needs to take care of her. Simon insists this is not a good time for them to take care of Eden's mother. Simon and Eden discuss the matter and come to an understanding. Eden challenges Simon on the man he has become. Simon finally confesses the mess he is in and the possibility of him going to jail, their losing their home and him possibly losing him life. Eden insists its due to Simon's self-reliance and distancing himself from God.

Andrew comes to Simon with the great news that he has seen the Messiah. Simon wants nothing to do with it. If the Messiah is not rich or a healer, Simon feels he could not be of much help to him. In desperation, Simon goes out fishing one last night having been informed by Matthew that Quintus would be coming after him at sunrise the next day.

Simon fishes and catches nothing. He has a soul-searching conversation with God out loud on the boat. Before the night is over, at the request of Eden, Andrew, James, John and Zebedee go out to fish with Simon to no avail. They catch nothing. Matthew spends the night on the beach recording this failure. When they come to the shore in the morning, they see a crowd at the beach. They think they're seeing Roman soldiers in waiting, but it's actually Jesus and a group listening to him.

Andrew points out to Simon, that it is Jesus the Messiah. Jesus has to convince Simon to stay and listen to his message. Simon reluctantly follows Jesus' order to cast the nets into the water. Jesus does a miracle with the fish. Simon acknowledges that Jesus is the Messiah. Jesus calls Simon, Andrew, James and John to come follow him. Matthew is in astonishment at what has happened. There is more than enough fish to pay off the debt that Simon owed.

Scriptures Woven Into Episode 4

4 John's clothes were made of camel's hair, and he had a leather belt around his waist. His food was locusts and wild honey. 5 People went out to him from Jerusalem and all Judea and the whole region of the Jordan. 6 Confessing their sins, they were baptized by him in the Jordan River.

7 But when he saw many of the Pharisees and Sadducees coming to where he was baptizing, he said to them: "You brood of vipers! Who warned you to flee from the coming wrath? 8 Produce fruit in keeping with repentance. 9 And do not think you can say to yourselves, 'We have Abraham as our father.' I tell you that out of these stones God can raise up children for Abraham. 10 The ax is already at the root of the trees, and every tree that does not produce good fruit will be cut down and thrown into the fire. *The New International Version* (Grand Rapids, MI: Zondervan, 2011), Mt 3:4–10.

35 The next day John was there again with two of his disciples. 36 When he saw Jesus passing by, he said, "Look, the Lamb of God!" 37 When the two disciples heard him say this, they followed Jesus. 38 Turning around, Jesus saw them following and asked, "What do you want?" They said, "Rabbi" (which means "Teacher"), "where are you staying?" 39 "Come," he replied, "and you will see." So they went and saw where he was staying, and they spent that day with him. It was about four in the afternoon. 40 Andrew, Simon Peter's brother, was one of the two who heard what John had said and who had followed Jesus. 41 The first thing Andrew did was to find his brother Simon and tell him, "We have found the Messiah" (that is, the Christ). *The New International Version* (Grand Rapids, MI: Zondervan, 2011), Jn 1:35–41.

11 He replied, "Because the knowledge of the secrets of the kingdom of heaven has been given to you, but not to them. 12 Whoever has will be given more, and they will have an abundance. Whoever does not have, even what

they have will be taken from them. 13 This is why I speak to them in parables: "Though seeing, they do not see; though hearing, they do not hear or understand." *The New International Version* (Grand Rapids, MI: Zondervan, 2011), Mt 13:11–13.

47 "Once again, the kingdom of heaven is like a net that was let down into the lake and caught all kinds of fish. 48 When it was full, the fishermen pulled it up on the shore. Then they sat down and collected the good fish in baskets, but threw the bad away. 49 This is how it will be at the end of the age. The angels will come and separate the wicked from the righteous 50 and throw them into the blazing furnace, where there will be weeping and gnashing of teeth." *The New International Version* (Grand Rapids, MI: Zondervan, 2011), Mt 13:47–50.

One day as Jesus was standing by the Lake of Gennesaret, the people were crowding around him and listening to the word of God. 2 He saw at the water's edge two boats, left there by the fishermen, who were washing their nets. 3 He got into one of the boats, the one belonging to Simon, and asked him to put out a little from shore. Then he sat down and taught the people from the boat. 4 When he had finished speaking, he said to Simon, "Put out into deep water, and let down the nets for a catch." 5 Simon answered, "Master, we've worked hard all night and haven't caught anything. But because you say so, I will let down the nets." 6 When they had done so, they caught such a large number of fish that their nets began to break. 7 So they signaled their partners in the other boat to come and help them, and they came and filled both boats so full that they began to sink. 8 When Simon Peter saw this, he fell at Jesus' knees and said, "Go away from me, Lord; I am a sinful man!" 9 For he and all his companions were astonished at the catch of fish they had taken, 10 and so were James and John, the sons of Zebedee, Simon's partners. Then Jesus said to Simon, "Don't be afraid; from now on you will fish for people." 11 So they pulled their boats up on shore, left everything and followed him. *The New International Version* (Grand Rapids, MI: Zondervan, 2011), Lk 5:1–11.

Biblical Characters Who Are Part of Episode 4
The Rock On Which It Is Built

John The Baptist

Although John is in prison, this is not the imprisonment that is recorded in the Scriptures. There is nothing to indicate a prior imprisonment than the one carried out Herod.

Matthew The Tax Collector

Matthew is a tax collector and does his job well. There is nothing recorded in Scripture on Matthew's conversations with the Romans nor of Matthew's spying on Simon and Andrew. This is the author's way of adding depth to what the life of a tax collector may have been.

Nicodemus The Pharisee

Nicodemus is an actual biblical character, however the Scriptures do not provide us with any facts concerning his life until he meets with Jesus at night in John chapter three. The author is helping us to understand why Nicodemus may have been so eager to meet with Jesus.

Andrew & Simon

The Scriptures do record Andrew and Simon are brothers and fishermen. The Scriptures also record that Andrew had first been a disciple of John the Baptist and that he tried to tell Simon about Jesus being the Son of God. The Scriptures do not record the plot of Simon working with the Romans to catch fishermen fishing on the Sabbath or any of the events surrounding the plot. The Scriptures do record Simon's interactions with Jesus on casting his nets into the water and the results which followed.

Simon's Wife (Eden)

Although the Scriptures indicate Peter was married, his wife's name is never mentioned. Eden is the name assigned to her by the authors of the chosen. The Scriptures do not record the interactions between Simon and his wife. The author has done this to add depth to the characters. Her mother's illness is recorded in the Scriptures.

James & John

The Scriptures do record James and John as brothers and as fishermen. They are recorded as coming to the aid of Simon and Andrew with the large catch of fish. They do leave their job as fishermen behind to follow Jesus.

Zebedee

The Scriptures do record Zebedee as the father of James and John and that he is also a fisherman. The Scriptures do not record the plot of fishermen fishing on the Sabbath, so none of the events concerning Zebedee around the plot are actual events. The author has done this to add depth to the characters.

Jesus

The Scriptures do record Jesus teaching the people. Jesus does have a conversation with Simon on the use of his boat. Jesus does tell Simon to put his nets back out and the miracle of the fish takes place. Jesus does call Simon, Andrew, James and John to come and follow him.

Bible Study Discussion Questions Episode 4
The Rock On Which It Is Built

1. What goes wrong for Simon on his first night out to help the Romans catch a group of illegal fishermen on the Sabbath?

2. Have you ever had a plan you thought you could get away with, and something went wrong immediately with the execution?

3. What price did Simon have to pay for his deception in the boat? Is it possible to know the full price we will have to pay when we choose to make bad choices?

4. Do you think the fishermen should have been willing to help Simon out with their catch since Simon had prevented their arrest and imprisonment? Why do you feel this way?

5. Why do you think Matthew is so eager to help Quintus to nail Simon?

6. Why were the Pharisees upset with John The Baptist?

7. Why do you think Simon is reluctant to joyfully receive his mother-in-law into their home? Do you feel more compassion for Simon or Eden in this situation? Why?

8. Do you think Eden is correct in identifying her husband's real problem is a spiritual one?

9. How can we tell if the root of a problem in our lives is actually a spiritual one that may be manifesting itself in other ways?

10. Why is Andrew excited about the discovery of Jesus as the "Lamb of God" and Simon could seem to care less?

11. How do our circumstances cause us to miss God when God may be right in front of us? How can fellow believers help us with this?

12. Why do you think Nicodemus is so concerned about John being put in prison?

13. In the dialogue between Matthew and Simon, what quality trait does Matthew recognize in Simon, that's missing in his own life?

14. If you were Simon, how would you feel towards Matthew knowing that he is following you around and spying on you for the Romans?

15. Simon was out on the lake in the boat in the dark by himself with no fish. Do you think Simon's honest talk with how he felt about God had any impact on him or on God?

16. What emotions did you experience when the nets filled up with fish and the other fishermen came running to the aid of Simon and Andrew?

17. How did Simon respond to this miracle of the fish? How much faith did Simon have prior to the miracle?

18. Why does God appear to require faith from some, but not from others to perform a miracle?

5 RESOURCES FOR EPISODE 5
THE WEDDING GIFT

Episode 5
The Wedding Gift
55 Minutes Viewing Time
The Main Characters

Jesus At 12—the episode begins with Jesus as a 12 year old the day his parents find him in the temple.

Mary—Jesus' mother finds him in Jerusalem. She also helps her friend to prepare for the wedding in Cana.

Joseph—Jesus's father finds Jesus in the temple as a 12 year old teaching the scribes and Pharisees.

Dinah and Ezra—the parents of the groom. They are from a poorer working family and struggle to cover the expenses of the wedding.

Killah and Abner—the parents of the bride. They are from an upper-class family and were not happy with their daughter's choice of a husband because of his background.

Nicodemus—the Pharisee who visits John the Baptist in prison. Nicodemus is on a search for truth for what God might being doing.

John The Baptist—the preacher who is in prison, but he thinks the Pharisees had him arrested. This is not the prison story in which Herod later has John arrested.

Simon—having been called by Jesus to follow him, Simon goes to share this new calling with his wife.

Eden—Simon's wife recognizes why Jesus called Simon to follow Him.

Thomas—a businessman who sells wine for weddings and parties. He is a disciplined planner and likes to plan for all contingencies in case something goes wrong. A very practical person.

Rhema—a young woman who is a partner with Thomas in his business. She tries to keep Thomas from worrying about what might go wrong.

Andrew, Simon, Big James, John, Thaddeus, James & Mary Magdalene—these are the followers of Jesus that accompany Jesus to the wedding.

Jesus—invites his followers to the wedding with him. Jesus resists doing a miracle in this situation because "His time has not yet come."

Summary Of Episode 5 The Wedding Gift

The episode starts in Jerusalem when Jesus would have been 12 years old. Mary races through the streets of Jerusalem searching for her son who has been gone for about 3 days. Joseph finds him teaching the scribes in the temple. Jesus is puzzled that his parents had been searching for him. Mary lets him know that "now is not the time" for Him to act like this, to which Jesus responds, "if not now, then when." The three of them both know that a change in their lives is coming.

The episode shifts about 18 years in time right after Jesus had called Simon, Andrew, James, and John to follow him after the miraculous catch of fish. The location of the scene is in Cana of Galilee in where preparations are being made for a wedding. The mother of the groom and Mary, Jesus' mother, are very close friends. Mary arrives early for the wedding to assist her friend Dinah with the preparations.

The parents of the groom are Dinah and Ezra. They are from the lower economic status and they are operating on a very limited financial budget for the wedding. The parents of the groom Killah and Abner are from an upper-class family, and they are not that happy with their daughter marrying a man from the lower class. Yet they know their daughter is in love with her fiancé.

Meanwhile, Nicodemus goes to John the Baptist who is in prison to try to get John to answer some questions. John tries to tell Nicodemus what his job is, but they have a dispute over words so this discussion is not very fruitful. This imprisonment of John the Baptist is not to be confused with the imprisonment that's done later by King

Herod.

Simon goes home and tries to explain to his wife what change took place in his life when the boat filled up with fish. He doesn't know how to tell his wife, Eden, that Jesus has told him to come and follow him. He thinks she may object to the call. Eden surprises Simon with her response to his call by Jesus.

Thomas is introduced as a businessman who is overly conservative in his actions because he wants things to work perfectly. He tends to look at what might go wrong, and wants to be prepared for it in advance. He is heavily dependent on the facts in a situation before making a decision. The Scriptures do not tell us about the circumstances of how Jesus and Thomas met. Although he is a real Biblical character, this introduction of him into the story of the water to wine miracle is not found in Scripture. The story does help us to understand why Thomas could have behaved in the manner he did after becoming a disciple of Jesus.

Rhema is introduced as either an assistant or helper of Thomas in the wine business of serving at weddings and parties. She has more faith that things will work out, even when one doesn't plan for what could go wrong.

The disciples that Jesus have called to follow him are all nervous, because they have no idea what that really means. They don't know whether to bring along food, clothing or what. One sees the tension of "what do we do next" as they gather to follow Jesus. When they are together, since Jesus has called two men with the name of James, he decides to call one of them Big James, since he is much taller than the other one.

Jesus and his disciples are invited to a wedding that is already operating on a limited budget. Thomas and Rhema were told there would be 40 guests present, but at least 80 have shown up. They were prepared to cover the 40 and even up to 60 but definitely not 80. They begin to run out of wine and to run out of options.

This will be a humiliating social and religious blow for Dinah and Ezra to run out of wine. Mary goes to her son, Jesus for help. She can't bear to see the embarrassment her best friend would suffer if the wedding party ended because there was no more wine. Jesus tells his mother, "my time has not yet come." Mary quotes back his own words to him what Jesus had said to her in the opening of the episode as a 12 year old, "If not now, then when." Mary tells the servants to do whatever Jesus tells them to do. Thomas doesn't believe there is anything Jesus can do to help this situation. Rhema is willing to do whatever Jesus says for them to do.

Jesus turns the water into wine when no one else is present in the room. Everyone is shocked at the quality of the wine. Even Ezra has a change of heart. Thomas is the most profoundly impacted by what Jesus has done. Jesus gives him the invitation to come and follow him. Thomas is not sure what he should do. Rhema tells Thomas, "maybe for once in your life, don't think." Thomas has 12 days to make a decision.

Scriptures Woven Into Episode 5 The Wedding Gift

41 Every year Jesus' parents went to Jerusalem for the Festival of the Passover. 42 When he was twelve years old, they went up to the festival, according to the custom. 43 After the festival was over, while his parents were returning home, the boy Jesus stayed behind in Jerusalem, but they were unaware of it. 44 Thinking he was in their

company, they traveled on for a day. Then they began looking for him among their relatives and friends. 45 When they did not find him, they went back to Jerusalem to look for him. 46 After three days they found him in the temple courts, sitting among the teachers, listening to them and asking them questions. 47 Everyone who heard him was amazed at his understanding and his answers. 48 When his parents saw him, they were astonished. His mother said to him, "Son, why have you treated us like this? Your father and I have been anxiously searching for you." 49 "Why were you searching for me?" he asked. "Didn't you know I had to be in my Father's house?" 50 But they did not understand what he was saying to them. 51 Then he went down to Nazareth with them and was obedient to them. But his mother treasured all these things in her heart. 52 And Jesus grew in wisdom and stature, and in favor with God and man. *The New International Version* (Grand Rapids, MI: Zondervan, 2011), Lk 2:41–52.

19 So Elijah went from there and found Elisha son of Shaphat. He was plowing with twelve yoke of oxen, and he himself was driving the twelfth pair. Elijah went up to him and threw his cloak around him. 20 Elisha then left his oxen and ran after Elijah. "Let me kiss my father and mother goodbye," he said, "and then I will come with you." "Go back," Elijah replied. "What have I done to you?" 21 So Elisha left him and went back. He took his yoke of oxen and slaughtered them. He burned the plowing equipment to cook the meat and gave it to the people, and they ate. Then he set out to follow Elijah and became his servant. *The New International Version* (Grand Rapids, MI: Zondervan, 2011), 1 Ki 19:19–21.

On the third day a wedding took place at Cana in Galilee. Jesus' mother was there, 2 and Jesus and his disciples had also been invited to the wedding. 3 When the wine was gone, Jesus' mother said to him, "They have no more wine." 4 "Woman, why do you involve me?" Jesus replied. "My hour has not yet come." 5 His mother said to the servants, "Do whatever he tells you." 6 Nearby stood six stone water jars, the kind used by the Jews for ceremonial washing, each holding from twenty to thirty gallons. 7 Jesus said to the servants, "Fill the jars with water"; so they filled them to the brim. 8 Then he told them, "Now draw some out and take it to the master of the banquet." They did so, 9 and the master of the banquet tasted the water that had been turned into wine. He did not realize where it had come from, though the servants who had drawn the water knew. Then he called the bridegroom aside 10 and said, "Everyone brings out the choice wine first and then the cheaper wine after the guests have had too much to drink; but you have saved the best till now." 11 What Jesus did here in Cana of Galilee was the first of the signs through which he revealed his glory; and his disciples believed in him. 12 After this he went down to Capernaum with his mother and brothers and his disciples. There they stayed for a few days. *The New International Version* (Grand Rapids, MI: Zondervan, 2011), Jn 2:1–12.

Biblical Characters Who Are Part Of Episode 5 The Wedding Gift

Mary & Joseph
The Scriptures do record Mary and Joseph looking for their son and finding him 3 days later at the temple. The

Scriptures also record Mary conversing with Jesus and asking for his help when they run out of wine at the wedding in Cana. The Scriptures do not record Mary assisting her friend at the wedding or any of their conversations.

Jesus As Twelve Year Old
The Scripture do record Jesus visiting the temple at age 12 and teaching the Scribes at the temple.

Jesus
The Scriptures do record Jesus performing the miracle of turning the water into wine and the episode portrays what the Scriptures says about the event. The interaction between Jesus and Thomas is not recorded in the Scriptures.

Andrew, Simon, James, John, James, Thaddaeus and Mary
Jesus' disciples were present at the wedding in Cana. The events in the episode around the wedding are not recorded in the Scriptures.

Mary Magdalene
Mary is recorded in the Scriptures as one of the followers of Jesus, but the Scriptures do not record her presence at the wedding, though she may have been there.

Nicodemus The Pharisee
Nicodemus is present in the Scriptures. The scenes of Nicodemus and John the Baptist are not recorded in the Scriptures.

John The Baptist
John the Baptist is recorded in the Scriptures. The Scriptures do not record John being in prison and having a discussion with Nicodemus. John's imprisonment will occur at a later time at the direction of Herod.

Andrew & Simon
Andrew and Simon are recorded in the Scriptures as brothers and among the first of the disciples called by Jesus. He is most likely among those at the wedding, but the Scriptures do not record any of his dialogue in this episode.

Simon's Wife (Eden)
Although the Scriptures indicate Simon was married, his wife's name is never mentioned. Eden is the name assigned to her by the authors of the Chosen. The Scriptures do not record any of the conversations between Simon and his wife.

Thomas
Thomas is a biblical character who will eventually become one of the Twelve. The Scriptures are silent on the manner in which Jesus and Thomas meet. The Scriptures do not record Thomas as having a role in the wedding at Cana.

Bible Study Questions Episode 5 The Wedding Gift

1. How do you think Mary and Joseph felt knowing that for 3 days, not only had they lost their own son, they had also lost the Son of God who was to become the Savior of the world?

2. What do you think would have been the most difficult part for Mary after her husband Joseph died?

3. Why do Nicodemus and John have such a difficult time having a decent conversation in the prison?

4. Do you think Dinah and Ezra planned for a more elaborate wedding than they should have? What do you think was Dinah's hope?

5. Have you ever planned for something big and had to settle for less because of your finances? How did you handle it?

6. Why did Eden react in the manner she did when Peter shared His calling from Jesus?

7. Who in your life saw something positive in you before you could see it in yourself?

8. What do we learn about Thomas, the future disciple, from the way he is portrayed in this episode?

9. What do you think you would have brought along if Jesus told you to come and follow him, but he didn't say for how long or where you were going? What would be going through your head?

10. Mary said the disciples would know what to do by watching Him, again and again. How do we watch Jesus today?

11. What is it about Abner, the bride's father that turns you off? Have you ever prejudged someone because of their background or appearance?

12. Why does Simon seem more ready to launch Jesus's ministry than Jesus does? What causes us to sometimes want to get ahead of God in what God wants to do in our lives?

13. Would you have been tempted to hide the truth about running out of wine from the banquet master? What's on the line for Thomas & Rhema?

14. What is it that tempts us to lie or to conceal the truth?

15. What motivates Mary to plead with Jesus to do something?

16. What's the conflict going on inside of Jesus because of his mother's request?

17. How do you think Ezra and Dinah were feeling, when the banquet master said he had an announcement to make?

18. Have you ever had a situation in which all hope seemed lost, and just at the last minute, God changed your situation.

19. Why does it seem as though Abner had a change of heart after drinking the wine?

20. Why is Thomas having a difficult time with the miracle and Jesus' invitation?

6 RESOURCES FOR EPISODE 6
INDECRIBABLE COMPASSION

Episode 6   Indescribable Compassion
52 Minutes Viewing Time

The Main Characters:

The Leper—the person attempting to sell items at pawn shop and then encounters Jesus on the roadside.

Matthew—the tax collector who is touched by having seen the miracle Jesus did with the fishes.

Gaius—the Roman guard who watches over Matthew and seeks to maintain the peace in Capernaum.

Quintus—The Roman leader who seeks advice from Matthew.

Nicodemus—the Pharisee who gives a   to the Council on his visit with John The Baptist and desperately wants to meet with Jesus.

Shmuel—the rabbi student of Nicodemus who thinks both John the Baptist and Jesus are a threat.

Tamar—an Ethiopian woman who grew up in Egypt and sees Jesus heal the leper.

Zebedee & Salome—parents of James and John and the healing takes place in their home.

Simon—insists on being a body guard for Jesus.

Mary Magdalene—attempts to help Tamar and her friends as well as agrees to help Nicodemus meet Jesus.

Jesus—the leader of the disciples and the compassionate teacher who heals the leper and the lame man.

Summary of Episode 6 Indescribable Compassion

The episode begins with a group of people waiting in line at a pawn shop. One man goes in with a number of items under his coat. The pawn shop owner thinks the items are stolen, so he tries to take advantage of the man by offering him a very low price. In the ensuing discussion, the man's clothing moves and reveals he is a leper. The pawn shop owner insists that he get out of his store.

The episode then moves to the marketplace with Matthew and Gaius guarding the immense sum of money that came from selling the fish that Peter had caught when he followed Jesus' command to cast out his net. Later, Matthew tries to explain what happened with the catch of fish, but Quintus is only interested in how he can exploit the situation. This discussion is interrupted by the news that a rival of Quintus would be in town in an hour and Quintus is not sure how to impress this rival. He gives Matthew a hypothetical to which Matthew provides a great insight. Quintus puts Matthew's plan into action

The scene changes to Nicodemus giving a report to the Council on his visit with John the Baptist. He insists the John that Baptist is more of a misguided rogue preacher than anything else and not a threat to them or to Rome. Rabbi Shmuel is the one who had John arrested. Nicodemus and Shmuel will begin to clash with one another several times throughout the episode on the interpretation of the Torah.

The disciples are learning what it means to travel on the road as they break camp. Jesus sends Simon to leave the group early to take care of matters back home. Simon's mother-in-law is sick. As Jesus and the disciples are walking on the road, Jesus meets a woman from Ethiopia named Tamar. Tamar grew up in Egypt. Jesus speaks to her in Egyptian and lets her know his childhood was spent in Egypt and her necklace reminded him of things he had seen there.

As the conversation ends, the leper who was first introduced at the opening of the episode comes down the road. The disciples demand that he keep his distance away from Jesus. Yet Jesus goes to the leper, and the leper falls to his feet. Jesus heals the leper and the process is seen by the disciples and by Tamar. Jesus insists the leper not tell anyone what he has done, but rather to follow the law of Moses for the cleansing of a leper.

The scene then goes to the house of Zebedee and Salome. They welcome their sons, James and John, and Jesus and other disciples into their home. A crowd gathers at their home, and Jesus begins teaching. The more he teaches, the larger the crowd becomes. Simon is afraid the size of the crowd could lead to trouble. Gaius closes Matthew's booth because he gets news of a crowd growing in another section of the city because of a preacher. Matthew suspects it might be Jesus and insists on going along with them. Nicodemus, Rabbi Shmuel and Rabbi Joseph all rush to the area as well.

Tamar returns with her friends, one of who is a paralytic, in order to get him to Jesus for a healing. They can't get anywhere near the door. So they take their friend to the roof, to lower him down to Jesus. Tamar asks Jesus to do for her friend what she saw him do for the leper.

Matthew finds a seat on a roof with two youths, Abigail and Joshua the Brave, who had met Jesus in an earlier episode. Once Jesus heals the lame man, people have a host of different reactions. Some praise God, but Rabbi Shmuel calls for the Roman soldiers. Jesus and the disciples are forced to escape from the house through a back alley. Nicodemus begs Mary to get him a meeting with Jesus. Matthew realizes that he is truly lost and does not know what to do.

Scriptures Woven Into Episode 6 Indescribable Compassion

One day as Jesus was standing by the Lake of Gennesaret, the people were crowding around him and listening to the word of God. 2 He saw at the water's edge two boats, left there by the fishermen, who were washing their nets. 3 He got into one of the boats, the one belonging to Simon, and asked him to put out a little from shore. Then he sat down and taught the people from the boat. 4 When he had finished speaking, he said to Simon, "Put out into deep water, and let down the nets for a catch." 5 Simon answered, "Master, we've worked hard all night and haven't caught anything. But because you say so, I will let down the nets." 6 When they had done so, they caught such a large number of fish that their nets began to break. 7 So they signaled their partners in the other boat to come and help them, and they came and filled both boats so full that they began to sink. 8 When Simon Peter saw this, he fell at Jesus' knees and said, "Go away from me, Lord; I am a sinful man!" 9 For he and all his companions were astonished at the catch of fish they had taken, 10 and so were James and John, the sons of Zebedee, Simon's partners. Then Jesus said to Simon, "Don't be afraid; from now on you will fish for people." 11 So they pulled their boats up on shore, left everything and followed him *The New International Version* (Grand Rapids, MI: Zondervan, 2011), Lk 5:1–11.

13 When they had gone, an angel of the Lord appeared to Joseph in a dream. "Get up," he said, "take the child and his mother and escape to Egypt. Stay there until I tell you, for Herod is going to search for the child to kill him." 14 So he got up, took the child and his mother during the night and left for Egypt, 15 where he stayed until the death of Herod. And so was fulfilled what the Lord had said through the prophet: "Out of Egypt I called my son." 16 When Herod realized that he had been outwitted by the Magi, he was furious, and he gave orders to kill all the boys in Bethlehem and its vicinity who were two years old and under, in accordance with the time he had learned from the Magi. 17 Then what was said through the prophet Jeremiah was fulfilled: 18 "A voice is heard in Ramah,

weeping and great mourning, Rachel weeping for her children and refusing to be comforted, because they are no more." The Return to Nazareth 19 After Herod died, an angel of the Lord appeared in a dream to Joseph in Egypt 20 and said, "Get up, take the child and his mother and go to the land of Israel, for those who were trying to take the child's life are dead." 21 So he got up, took the child and his mother and went to the land of Israel. 22 But when he heard that Archelaus was reigning in Judea in place of his father Herod, he was afraid to go there. Having been warned in a dream, he withdrew to the district of Galilee, 23 and he went and lived in a town called Nazareth. *The New International Version* (Grand Rapids, MI: Zondervan, 2011), Mt 2:13–23.

12 While Jesus was in one of the towns, a man came along who was covered with leprosy. When he saw Jesus, he fell with his face to the ground and begged him, "Lord, if you are willing, you can make me clean." 13 Jesus reached out his hand and touched the man. "I am willing," he said. "Be clean!" And immediately the leprosy left him. 14 Then Jesus ordered him, "Don't tell anyone, but go, show yourself to the priest and offer the sacrifices that Moses commanded for your cleansing, as a testimony to them." *The New International Version* (Grand Rapids, MI: Zondervan, 2011), Lk 5:12–14.

5 The whole Judean countryside and all the people of Jerusalem went out to him. Confessing their sins, they were baptized by him in the Jordan River. 6 John wore clothing made of camel's hair, with a leather belt around his waist, and he ate locusts and wild honey. 7 And this was his message: "After me comes the one more powerful

than I, the straps of whose sandals I am not worthy to stoop down and untie. 8 I baptize you with water, but he will baptize you with the Holy Spirit." *The New International Version* (Grand Rapids, MI: Zondervan, 2011), Mk 1:5–8.

Once again, the kingdom of heaven is like a net that was let down into the lake and caught all kinds of fish. 48 When it was full, the fishermen pulled it up on the shore. Then they sat down and collected the good fish in baskets, but threw the bad away. 49 This is how it will be at the end of the age. The angels will come and separate the wicked from the righteous 50 and throw them into the blazing furnace, where there will be weeping and gnashing of teeth. *The New International Version* (Grand Rapids, MI: Zondervan, 2011), Mt 13:47–50.

"But about that day or hour no one knows, not even the angels in heaven, nor the Son, but only the Father. 37 As it was in the days of Noah, so it will be at the coming of the Son of Man. 38 For in the days before the flood, people were eating and drinking, marrying and giving in marriage, up to the day Noah entered the ark; 39 and they knew nothing about what would happen until the flood came and took them all away. That is how it will be at the coming of the Son of Man. 40 Two men will be in the field; one will be taken and the other left. 41 Two women will be grinding with a hand mill; one will be taken and the other left. 42 "Therefore keep watch, because you do not know on what day your Lord will come. 43 But understand this: If the owner of the house had known at what time of night the thief was coming, he would have kept watch and would not have let his house be broken into. 44 So you also must be ready, because the Son of

Man will come at an hour when you do not expect him. 45 "Who then is the faithful and wise servant, whom the master has put in charge of the servants in his household to give them their food at the proper time? 46 It will be good for that servant whose master finds him doing so when he returns. 47 Truly I tell you, he will put him in charge of all his possessions. 48 But suppose that servant is wicked and says to himself, 'My master is staying away a long time,' 49 and he then begins to beat his fellow servants and to eat and drink with drunkards. 50 The master of that servant will come on a day when he does not expect him and at an hour he is not aware of. 51 He will cut him to pieces and assign him a place with the hypocrites, where there will be weeping and gnashing of teeth. *The New International Version* (Grand Rapids, MI: Zondervan, 2011), Mt. 24:36-51

Now there were some present at that time who told Jesus about the Galileans whose blood Pilate had mixed with their sacrifices. 2 Jesus answered, "Do you think that these Galileans were worse sinners than all the other Galileans because they suffered this way? 3 I tell you, no! But unless you repent, you too will all perish. 4 Or those eighteen who died when the tower in Siloam fell on them—do you think they were more guilty than all the others living in Jerusalem? 5 I tell you, no! But unless you repent, you too will all perish." *The New International Version* (Grand Rapids, MI: Zondervan, 2011), Lk 13:1–5.

2 "So when you give to the needy, do not announce it with trumpets, as the hypocrites do in the synagogues and on the streets, to be honored by others. Truly I tell you, they

have received their reward in full. 3 But when you give to the needy, do not let your left hand know what your right hand is doing, 4 so that your giving may be in secret. Then your Father, who sees what is done in secret, will reward you. Prayer 6:9–13pp—Lk 11:2–4 5 "And when you pray, do not be like the hypocrites, for they love to pray standing in the synagogues and on the street corners to be seen by others. Truly I tell you, they have received their reward in full. 6 But when you pray, go into your room, close the door and pray to your Father, who is unseen. Then your Father, who sees what is done in secret, will reward you. 7 And when you pray, do not keep on babbling like pagans, for they think they will be heard because of their many words. 8 Do not be like them, for your Father knows what you need before you ask him. *The New International Version* (Grand Rapids, MI: Zondervan, 2011), Mt 6:2–8.

Jesus told this parable: 10 "Two men went up to the temple to pray, one a Pharisee and the other a tax collector. 11 The Pharisee stood by himself and prayed: 'God, I thank you that I am not like other people—robbers, evildoers, adulterers—or even like this tax collector. 12 I fast twice a week and give a tenth of all I get.' 13 "But the tax collector stood at a distance. He would not even look up to heaven, but beat his breast and said, 'God, have mercy on me, a sinner.' 14 "I tell you that this man, rather than the other, went home justified before God. For all those who exalt themselves will be humbled, and those who humble themselves will be exalted *The New International Version* (Grand Rapids, MI: Zondervan, 2011), Lk 18:9–14.

A few days later, when Jesus again entered Capernaum, the people heard that he had come home. 2 They gathered in such large numbers that there was no room left, not even outside the door, and he preached the word to them. 3 Some men came, bringing to him a paralyzed man, carried by four of them. 4 Since they could not get him to Jesus because of the crowd, they made an opening in the roof above Jesus by digging through it and then lowered the mat the man was lying on. 5 When Jesus saw their faith, he said to the paralyzed man, "Son, your sins are forgiven." 6 Now some teachers of the law were sitting there, thinking to themselves, 7 "Why does this fellow talk like that? He's blaspheming! Who can forgive sins but God alone?" 8 Immediately Jesus knew in his spirit that this was what they were thinking in their hearts, and he said to them, "Why are you thinking these things? 9 Which is easier: to say to this paralyzed man, 'Your sins are forgiven,' or to say, 'Get up, take your mat and walk'? 10 But I want you to know that the Son of Man has authority on earth to forgive sins." So he said to the man, 11 "I tell you, get up, take your mat and go home." 12 He got up, took his mat and walked out in full view of them all. This amazed everyone and they praised God, saying, "We have never seen anything like this! *The New International Version* (Grand Rapids, MI: Zondervan, 2011), Mk 2:1–12.

Biblical Characters Who Are Part Of Episode 6
Indescribable Compassion

The Man With Leprosy
2 A man with leprosy came and knelt before him and said, "Lord, if you are willing, you can make me clean." *The New International Version* (Grand Rapids, MI: Zondervan, 2011), Mt 8:1–2.

The Men Bringing In The Paralyzed Man and The Paralyzed Man

Some men came, bringing to him a paralyzed man, carried by four of them. 4 Since they could not get him to Jesus because of the crowd, they made an opening in the roof above Jesus by digging through it and then lowered the mat the man was lying on. *The New International Version* (Grand Rapids, MI: Zondervan, 2011), Mk 2:3–4.

Jesus' Early Youth

The Escape to Egypt 13 When they had gone, an angel of the Lord appeared to Joseph in a dream. "Get up," he said, "take the child and his mother and escape to Egypt. Stay there until I tell you, for Herod is going to search for the child to kill him." 14 So he got up, took the child and his mother during the night and left for Egypt, 15 where he stayed until the death of Herod. *The New International Version* (Grand Rapids, MI: Zondervan, 2011), Mt 2:13–15.

Andrew, Simon, James, John, James, Thaddaeus and Mary

One could assume from the context of Scripture that Jesus' disciples were with him for the healing of the man with leprosy and with the healing of the paralytic, but we have no record of any conversations they had at the time among themselves.

Nicodemus The Pharisee

Although Nicodemus is a biblical character, the bible does not identify him as being at the healing of the paralyzed man, but it does indicate some Pharisees were present at the event. It could be that Nicodemus was among them. The bible does not provide us with any of the words uttered by Nicodemus in this episode

Simon's Wife (Eden)

*(Although the Scriptures indicate Peter was married, his wife's name is never mentioned. Eden is the name assigned to her by the authors of the chosen) There is no mention in the Scriptures of the dialogue Eden has in this episode.

Jesus' Teachings

All of the teachings that Jesus provides in this episode can be found in the Scriptures. His healing of the man with leprosy and the healing of the man who had been paralyzed are consistent with the Scriptures. His confrontation with the Pharisees is also documented in the Scriptures.

Bible Study Questions Episode 6
Indescribable Compassion

1. What has been one of the most compassionate things that someone has done for you? How did it leave you feeling inside?

2. How do you think the man with leprosy in the opening of the episode felt knowing that he was being cheated, but there was nothing he could do about it?

3. Do you think Nicodemus is trying to protect John the Baptist in his report to the Council? Why or Why not?

4. Why do you think Peter laughed at the idea that Little James could have been in the choir in Jerusalem? Why do we misjudge the abilities of other so quickly?

5. Each episode gives us a different glimpse of Matthew. What do you learn about him in his dealings with Quintus?

6. Have you ever thought about Jesus' early childhood being spent in Africa? What does this tell us about God?

7. With all that Jesus has done for the disciples, why do you think they react so negatively to the man with leprosy coming down the road?

8. How did you feel when Jesus embraced the man who had had leprosy? When was a time you felt embraced by God?

9. Does following Jesus automatically make us more compassionate? Why or why not?

10. Why is Peter so angry with Matthew? Do you identify more with Peter or Matthew in their argument with each other?

11. Why does Nicodemus and Rabbi Shmuel have a hard time relating to each other in discussing the Torah?

12. How do we know when we simply have a disagreement over an interpretation of Scripture, and when a person has gone into error or false teaching?

13. The disciples have this need to "protect Jesus" from harm. How do we attempt to protect Jesus today?

14. What can we learn from Tamar in her bringing her friends to Jesus? What keeps us from having Tamar's boldness?

15. What emotion did you have when Tamar gasped at the healing of her friend or when the healed man held and hugged Jesus?

16. Why do you think Rabbi Shmuel called for the Roman guards?

17. What do you think Nicodemus was thinking when the healed man walked past him?

18. Why do you think Nicodemus wants a private talk with Jesus?

19. Abigail, the little girl, had asked Matthew if he was lost. What do you think Matthew is feeling, when he and Jesus look at each other at the end of the episode?

7 RESOURCES FOR EPISODE 7 INVITATIONS

Episode 7 Invitations
38 Minutes Viewing Time
The Main Characters

Moses & Joshua—the men at the beginning discussing the issue of Moses building a bronze snake.

Nicodemus & his wife--the couple discuss whether of not to return to Jerusalem so that Nicodemus can circumcise his newly born grandchild.

Quintus—Roman praetor who wants Nicodemus to betray Jesus.

Gaius & Matthew—the Roman guard who protects Matthew. Matthew is a successful tax collector who walks away from it all. Gaius believes Matthew is making a huge mistake.

Mary Magdalene-the disciple of Jesus who apologizes for

not keeping people away from him while he was teaching.

Jesus—the one who addresses Mary, meets with Nicodemus, and challenges Matthew.

Matthew's mother—the one who allows Matthew in her home and reminds him of the great potential he had as a boy.

Simon & Eden—the couple who do not want to trouble Jesus with their mother's illness.

John—the disciple who writes down as much of the conversation between Jesus and Nicodemus as he possibly could.

Summary of Episode 7 Invitations

The episode begins with a flashback in history at the time the children of Israel are wandering in the desert and are calling the manna God has given them "miserable food." God sends venomous snakes among them and the people are dying from the bites. God tells Moses to build a bronze snake so that the people could look upon it and live. In the episode, Joshua challenges Moses on whether or not Moses's actions are the right course of action especially since he is building a pagan symbol.

The scene switches to Matthew's house in which one can see the level of success he has reached. The Roman guard Gaius comes to escort Matthew to work so that he no longer is beaten or threatened enroute to the tax collector booth. The two of them will have several conversations dealing with Matthew's wealth, his family, and his response to follow Jesus throughout the episode.

The scene switches to Nicodemus and his wife. She's ready to leave Capernaum, but he is not. They have a new grandchild in Jerusalem, and she insists Nicodemus must be there to perform the circumcision. They have an unexpected guest in the form of the Roman praetor Quintus. Quintus has plans for Jesus, and he attempts to solicit Nicodemus' help to carry them out.

The disciples are shown with Jesus as they are apparently not happy with the constant moving from village to village. Breaking and setting up camp can be a bit tiresome. Jesus reminds them of why it was he came. Mary thinks she was out of place to interrupt Jesus' teachings when she attempted to help Tamar and the man who was paralyzed in the previous episode to get to Jesus. She offers a sincere apology.

Matthew goes to visit his mother in hopes of having someone to talk to who understands Jewish law. His plan for his life was being challenged by seeing the things Jesus was doing. Matthew's mother provides insight that Matthew was a child prodigy with amazing intellectual abilities. His family is struggling financially and Matthew offers to help. Their meeting does not end in the way Matthew had hoped.

Simon and Eden appear briefly with Jesus in their home. For some reason, they do not want Jesus to know about Eden's mother's condition who is very ill. Simon expresses his concern over the upcoming meeting between Jesus and Nicodemus.

Jesus and Nicodemus meet in secret at night. Nicodemus has a host of questions for Jesus. Jesus refers back to his mission being similar to Moses in that he would be lifted up, and people would only need to look at him and believe. After being in the presence of Jesus, Nicodemus feels as though he's standing on Holy Ground. He's honored to embrace Jesus. Jesus gives him a costly invitation.

Jesus makes a surprise invitation to a person which greatly upsets the disciples, Simon especially. Jesus tells the disciples to get use to "different." The episode concludes with a big party that is about to take place.

Scriptures Woven Into Episode 7 Invitations

4 They traveled from Mount Hor along the route to the Red Sea, to go around Edom. But the people grew impatient on the way; 5 they spoke against God and against Moses, and said, "Why have you brought us up out of Egypt to die in the wilderness? There is no bread! There is no water! And we detest this miserable food!" 6 Then the Lord sent venomous snakes among them; they bit the people and many Israelites died. 7 The people came to Moses and said, "We sinned when we spoke against the Lord and against you. Pray that the Lord will take the snakes away from us." So Moses prayed for the people. 8 The Lord said to Moses, "Make a snake and put it up on a pole; anyone who is bitten can look at it and live." 9 So Moses made a bronze snake and put it up on a pole. Then when anyone was bitten by a snake and looked at the bronze snake, they lived. *The New International Version* (Grand Rapids, MI: Zondervan, 2011), Nu 21:4–9.

38 Jesus replied, "Let us go somewhere else—to the nearby villages—so I can preach there also. That is why I have come." 39 So he traveled throughout Galilee,

preaching in their synagogues and driving out demons. *The New International Version* (Grand Rapids, MI: Zondervan, 2011), Mk 1:38–39.

14 When Jesus came into Peter's house, he saw Peter's mother-in-law lying in bed with a fever. . *The New International Version* (Grand Rapids, MI: Zondervan, 2011), Matthew 8:14.

Now there was a Pharisee, a man named Nicodemus who was a member of the Jewish ruling council. 2 He came to Jesus at night and said, "Rabbi, we know that you are a teacher who has come from God. For no one could perform the signs you are doing if God were not with him." 3 Jesus replied, "Very truly I tell you, no one can see the kingdom of God unless they are born again." 4 "How can someone be born when they are old?" Nicodemus asked. "Surely they cannot enter a second time into their mother's womb to be born!" 5 Jesus answered, "Very truly I tell you, no one can enter the kingdom of God unless they are born of water and the Spirit. 6 Flesh gives birth to flesh, but the Spirit gives birth to spirit. 7 You should not be surprised at my saying, 'You must be born again.' 8 The wind blows wherever it pleases. You hear its sound, but you cannot tell where it comes from or where it is going. So it is with everyone born of the Spirit." *The New International Version* (Grand Rapids, MI: Zondervan, 2011), Jn 3:1–8.

9 "How can this be?" Nicodemus asked. 10 "You are Israel's teacher," said Jesus, "and do you not understand these things? 11 Very truly I tell you, we speak of what we know, and we testify to what we have seen, but still you

people do not accept our testimony. 12 I have spoken to you of earthly things and you do not believe; how then will you believe if I speak of heavenly things? 13 No one has ever gone into heaven except the one who came from heaven—the Son of Man. 14 Just as Moses lifted up the snake in the wilderness, so the Son of Man must be lifted up, 15 that everyone who believes may have eternal life in him." *The New International Version* (Grand Rapids, MI: Zondervan, 2011), Jn 3:9–15.

16 For God so loved the world that he gave his one and only Son, that whoever believes in him shall not perish but have eternal life. 17 For God did not send his Son into the world to condemn the world, but to save the world through him. 18 Whoever believes in him is not condemned, but whoever does not believe stands condemned already because they have not believed in the name of God's one and only Son. 19 *The New International Version* (Grand Rapids, MI: Zondervan, 2011), Jn 3:16–19.

4 When the Lord saw that he had gone over to look, God called to him from within the bush, "Moses! Moses!" And Moses said, "Here I am." 5 "Do not come any closer," God said. "Take off your sandals, for the place where you are standing is holy ground." 6 Then he said, "I am the God of your father, the God of Abraham, the God of Isaac and the God of Jacob." At this, Moses hid his face, because he was afraid to look at God. *The New International Version* (Grand Rapids, MI: Zondervan, 2011), Ex 3:4–6.

8 Taste and see that the Lord is good; blessed is the one who takes refuge in him. *The New International Version* (Grand Rapids, MI: Zondervan, 2011), Ps 34:8.

9 As Jesus went on from there, he saw a man named Matthew sitting at the tax collector's booth. "Follow me," he told him, and Matthew got up and followed him. 10 While Jesus was having dinner at Matthew's house, many tax collectors and sinners came and ate with him and his disciples.*The New International Version* (Grand Rapids, MI: Zondervan, 2011), Mt 9:9–10.

Biblical Characters Who Are Part Of Episode 7
Invitations

Moses and Joshua
Moses and Joshua are both biblical characters found from Exodus through Joshua in the Bible. The story is true of Moses building a bronze snake so that the people could be healed, but this conversation between the two is not found in the scriptures.

Matthew
Matthew is found in several of the gospels as both a tax collector and disciple of Jesus Christ. The conversations between Matthew and Gaius are not found in the Scriptures, neither is the conversation between Matthew and his mother. Jesus's call to Matthew to come follow him is found in the Scriptures as well as Matthew's response.

Nicodemus
Nicodemus is an actual biblical character mentioned in John chapters, 3, 7, and 19. The conversations between

Nicodemus, his wife, and the Roman praetor Quintus are not found in the Scriptures. The discussion Nicodemus has with Jesus is very similar to what is portrayed in the gospel of John chapter 3.

Mary Magdalene

Mary is an actual Biblical character however the conversation she has with Jesus in this episode is not recorded in the Scriptures.

Simon, Eden, Mother in Law

Simon is an actual biblical character mentioned many times in the Scriptures and will eventually become Peter. The scriptures do not provide us with the name of Simon's wife, though she is called Eden in the story. The Scriptures do record that Simon's mother in law was sick and that Jesus visited their house. The conversations of Simon, Eden and Jesus are not part of the Scriptures.

Jesus

Jesus is an actual biblical characters mentioned throughout all the gospels and many of the other books in the New Testament. Many of the scenes of him in the episode are actually found in the Scriptures. Most of the words he speaks are quotations of the Scriptures. He does have a night meeting with Nicodemus. There is not a record of Jesus issuing an invitation for Nicodemus to come follow him. The story of Jesus issuing a call to Matthew to come and follow him is found in several of the gospels.

John and Andrew

John and Andrew are disciples of Jesus found in each of the four gospels. Although John is taking notes on the talk

Jesus is having with Nicodemus, this is not found in the Scriptures.

Bible Study Discussion Questions Episode 7
Invitations

1. What is one of the most important or significant invitations you have received in the natural world? How did your acceptance of it, change your life?

2. Do you think Joshua was wrong to challenge Moses on what he was doing building the snake on the pole based on the facts available to Joshua? Why are we sometimes reluctant to challenge leaders?

3. If you had been called to follow Jesus literally as the disciples in the episode had, what do you think would have been the most difficult part of the process for you? What would have been your greatest reward?

4. Why do you think Jesus seems to have such a need to go away by himself and pray? Why do many believers lack that same kind of a need?

5. How did you feel about the interactions that took place between Matthew and his mother? Has anyone ever let you know they were disappointed in you? How did you handle it?

6. What did you find out about Matthew that had not been revealed in earlier episodes?

7. Simon and Eden tried to hide their mother's condition from Jesus. Why do we sometimes think we should not bother God with certain concerns?

8. How big does an issue have to be for us to bring it to God? Why, and how did you reach that conclusion?

9. What type of kingdom do you think Jesus is establishing on the earth?

10. What impresses you the most about Nicodemus in his discussion with Jesus?

11. What is Nicodemus actually saying when he states that he feels as though he is standing on Holy Ground?

12. Jesus lists a host of things Nicodemus would be leaving behind if he came to be one of his disciples. What do you think is the hardest thing to leave behind in order to follow Jesus?

13. Are you encouraged or frightened by Jesus words that the Spirit may work in a way that is not expected?

14. What emotion came to your mind at the sight of Jesus and Nicodemus embracing each other?

15. Why do you think Jesus called Matthew, "Matthew Son of Alpheus" come follow me?

16. Why do you think Gaius tried so hard to make Matthew see all that he was giving up?

17. Why do you think the disciples, especially Simon, wants Jesus to reconsider the offer made to Matthew?

18. Why are we tempted to see the sins of others as more evil than our own?

19. How would you have felt if you were Matthew, knowing that even though Jesus called you, the others didn't want you in the group? How are we guilty of letting newcomers know that they are not fully welcome in our midst?

20. How would you feel if Jesus invited you to a small special dinner party only to arrive and discover a person you didn't get along well with had also

been invited and just the three of you were sitting at the same table?

8 RESOURCES FOR EPISODE 8 I AM HE

Episode 8 I Am He
60 Minutes Viewing Time

The Main Characters

Jacob and Hassib—the two men have a discussion on the quality of land Jacob has purchased from the sons of Hamor and a discussion on the kind of God that Jacob serves.

The Woman at the well and her husband—the woman goes to her husband for a divorce but he insists that she is property and will never give her a divorce. The woman later encounters Jesus.

Rabbi Joseph—one of the Pharisees who interrupts Matthew's party and is shocked at Jesus being in the home of tax collectors and sinners.

Gaius—the Roman soldier who seeks to get Matthew to stop following Jesus. He also informs Quintus of

Matthew's decision to quit and later visits Matthew's family.

Nicodemus and his wife- Nicodemus is to receive a high honor. His wife is proud of him and reminds him she loves their current lives back in Jerusalem. Nicodemus struggles with the call to follow Jesus.

Rabbi Shmuel—former student of Nicodemus who has plenty of political ambition among the Pharisees. He turns against Nicodemus.

Simon, Eden, and Mother-in-law.—Jesus visits their home to make it easier for Eden while Simon is away.

The Disciples—they all pack up and say goodbye leaving their homes behind. They have a hard time understanding some of the plans of Jesus and questions his directions.

Jesus—he gathers the disciples for their trip, heals a woman, breaks down the Jewish/Samaritan wall, and begins to make himself known publicly.

Summary of Episode 8 I AM HE

The episode goes back into the time of the patriarch, Jacob, in the book of Genesis. Jacob and his sons have purchased some land from the sons of Hamor and are digging a well in search of water. Jacob is locating the spot for his sons to begin digging for water, when a stranger, Hassib approaches. Hassib is convinced that the sons of Hamor have swindled Jacob out of his money for the land. Yet Jacob is convinced the hand of God is in the purchase of the land. Jacob uses the opportunity to share information about the kind of God he serves. Hassib is surprised to see water coming out of the well.

The scene switches to the time of Jesus almost two thousand years later. The woman seeks to draw water from the same well that Jacob is credited to have built. The woman is revealed as an outcast who is despised by others. She goes to her husband and begs him for a divorce since she is living with another man. Her husband, out of spite more than anything else, refuses to sign the papers for the divorce. He considers her his property, and will never give her up no matter what she does.

The scene then goes to Matthew's house where they are enjoying the party that Jesus promised when Matthew responded to Jesus' invitation to follow him. The first uninvited guests to show up are Rabbi Joseph and another teacher. They condemn Jesus for being at this party. Jesus shares some scriptures with them on what God truly wants from people. The second unexpected guest is Gaius. He wants Matthew to come back to his old job. Gaius agrees to do Matthew a favor before leaving the party.

The next scene is back with Nicodemus and his wife, as Nicodemus prepares to receive a high honor from his order. They have a discussion on the unexpected plans of God. His wife reminds Nicodemus that she loves the life they have back in Jerusalem and is eager to return to it.

Gaius has the unfortunate job of informing Quintus that Matthew has quit his job as tax collector. Quintus is not happy with the news, and is even more incensed to learn Matthew left to follow Jesus.

Quintus later issues an edict banning religious gathering outside of a school or synagogue. He makes it known that Jesus is wanted for questioning.

The presentation award ceremony goes well for Nicodemus. A congratulations from Rabbi Shmuel to Nicodemus ends in a confrontation between the two men. Rabbi Shmuel wants to specialize in false prophecy and he questions why Nicodemus had not challenged Jesus when Jesus referred to himself as the Son of Man at the time of healing the paralytic who had been lowered through the roof.

Jesus visits the home of Simon and Eden again. Andrew is also present. Jesus shares with Eden, the role she is to play in his ministry. Jesus goes in and heals Simon's mother in law. She is surprised by the people in the room and is unsure of who Jesus is. She immediately gets out of bed and starts to wait on everyone.

Everyone is shown saying goodbye to their homes, friends, or family in order to accompany Jesus on his journey. Nicodemus comes to the place where Jesus had asked them all to meet. Nicodemus cannot bring himself to leave everything and follow Jesus. He does try to help them out on their journey with a special gift. Both he and Jesus are saddened by Nicodemus's choice.

Jesus upsets the disciples with his decision to go through Samaria rather than around it. After spending the night in a village, the next day he sends the disciples ahead to get some food. He told them to meet him at the well. As he sits at the well, the woman from Samaria returns for water. She and Jesus have a discussion with each other that turns deeply spiritual.

By the time the discussion ends, she finds the love of God and Jesus reveals himself as the Messiah.

She wants to go and tell everyone about Jesus. The first group she runs into are the disciples coming back to Jesus. She informs them that Jesus is the Christ as she rushes into town to tell others. The disciples are excited to know that Jesus is ready to reveal himself to the world

Scriptures Woven Into Episode 8 "I AM HE"

6 Abram traveled through the land as far as the site of the great tree of Moreh at Shechem. At that time the Canaanites were in the land. 7 The Lord appeared to Abram and said, "To your offspring I will give this land." So he built an altar there to the Lord, who had appeared to him. *The New International Version* (Grand Rapids, MI: Zondervan, 2011), Ge 12:6–7.

18 After Jacob came from Paddan Aram, he arrived safely at the city of Shechem in Canaan and camped within sight of the city. 19 For a hundred pieces of silver, he bought from the sons of Hamor, the father of Shechem, the plot of ground where he pitched his tent. 20 There he set up an altar and called it El Elohe Israel *The New International Version* (Grand Rapids, MI: Zondervan, 2011), Ge 33:18–20.

24 So Jacob was left alone, and a man wrestled with him till daybreak. 25 When the man saw that he could not overpower him, he touched the socket of Jacob's hip so that his hip was wrenched as he wrestled with the man. 26 Then the man said, "Let me go, for it is daybreak." But Jacob replied, "I will not let you go

unless you bless me." 27 The man asked him, "What is your name?" "Jacob," he answered. 28 Then the man said, "Your name will no longer be Jacob, but Israel, because you have struggled with God and with humans and have overcome." 29 Jacob said, "Please tell me your name." But he replied, "Why do you ask my name?" Then he blessed him there. 30 So Jacob called the place Peniel, saying, "It is because I saw God face to face, and yet my life was spared." *The New International Version* (Grand Rapids, MI: Zondervan, 2011), Ge 32:24–30.

4 Now he had to go through Samaria. 5 So he came to a town in Samaria called Sychar, near the plot of ground Jacob had given to his son Joseph. 6 Jacob's well was there, and Jesus, tired as he was from the journey, sat down by the well. It was about noon. *The New International Version* (Grand Rapids, MI: Zondervan, 2011), Jn 4:4–6.

9 As Jesus went on from there, he saw a man named Matthew sitting at the tax collector's booth. "Follow me," he told him, and Matthew got up and followed him. 10 While Jesus was having dinner at Matthew's house, many tax collectors and sinners came and ate with him and his disciples. 11 When the Pharisees saw this, they asked his disciples, "Why does your teacher eat with tax collectors and sinners?" 12 On hearing this, Jesus said, "It is not the healthy who need a doctor, but the sick. 13 But go and learn what this means: 'I desire mercy, not sacrifice.' For I have not come to call the righteous, but sinners." *The New International Version* (Grand Rapids, MI: Zondervan,

2011), Mt 9:9–13.

6 For I desire mercy, not sacrifice, and acknowledgment of God rather than burnt offerings *The New International Version* (Grand Rapids, MI: Zondervan, 2011), Ho 6:6.

13 She gave this name to the Lord who spoke to her: "You are the God who sees me," for she said, "I have now seen the One who sees me." 14 That is why the well was called Beer Lahai Roi; it is still there, between Kadesh and Bered. 15 So Hagar bore Abram a son, and Abram gave the name Ishmael to the son she had borne. 16 Abram was eighty-six years old when Hagar bore him Ishmael. *The New International Version* (Grand Rapids, MI: Zondervan, 2011), Ge 16:13–16.

"In my vision at night I looked, and there before me was one like a son of man, coming with the clouds of heaven. He approached the Ancient of Days and was led into his presence. 14 He was given authority, glory and sovereign power; all nations and peoples of every language worshiped him. His dominion is an everlasting dominion that will not pass away, and his kingdom is one that will never be destroyed. *The New International Version* (Grand Rapids, MI: Zondervan, 2011), Da 7:13–14.

14 When Jesus came into Peter's house, he saw Peter's mother-in-law lying in bed with a fever. 15 He touched her hand and the fever left her, and she got up and began to wait on him. *The New International Version* (Grand Rapids, MI: Zondervan, 2011), Mt 8:14–15.

7 When a Samaritan woman came to draw water, Jesus said to her, "Will you give me a drink?" 8 (His disciples had gone into the town to buy food.) 9 The Samaritan woman said to him, "You are a Jew and I am a Samaritan woman. How can you ask me for a drink?" (For Jews do not associate with Samaritans.) 10 Jesus answered her, "If you knew the gift of God and who it is that asks you for a drink, you would have asked him and he would have given you living water." 11 "Sir," the woman said, "you have nothing to draw with and the well is deep. Where can you get this living water? 12 Are you greater than our father Jacob, who gave us the well and drank from it himself, as did also his sons and his livestock?" 13 Jesus answered, "Everyone who drinks this water will be thirsty again, 14 but whoever drinks the water I give them will never thirst. Indeed, the water I give them will become in them a spring of water welling up to eternal life." 15 The woman said to him, "Sir, give me this water so that I won't get thirsty and have to keep coming here to draw water." 16 He told her, "Go, call your husband and come back." 17 "I have no husband," she replied. Jesus said to her, "You are right when you say you have no husband. 18 The fact is, you have had five husbands, and the man you now have is not your husband. What you have just said is quite true." 19 "Sir," the woman said, "I can see that you are a prophet. 20 Our ancestors worshiped on this mountain, but you Jews claim that the place where we must worship is in Jerusalem." 21 "Woman," Jesus replied, "believe me, a time is coming when you will worship the Father neither on this mountain nor in Jerusalem. 22 You Samaritans worship what you do not know; we

worship what we do know, for salvation is from the Jews. 23 Yet a time is coming and has now come when the true worshipers will worship the Father in the Spirit and in truth, for they are the kind of worshipers the Father seeks. 24 God is spirit, and his worshipers must worship in the Spirit and in truth." 25 The woman said, "I know that Messiah" (called Christ) "is coming. When he comes, he will explain everything to us." 26 Then Jesus declared, "I, the one speaking to you—I am he." *The New International Version* (Grand Rapids, MI: Zondervan, 2011), Jn 4:7–26.

27 Just then his disciples returned and were surprised to find him talking with a woman. But no one asked, "What do you want?" or "Why are you talking with her?" 28 Then, leaving her water jar, the woman went back to the town and said to the people, 29 "Come, see a man who told me everything I ever did. Could this be the Messiah?" 30 They came out of the town and made their way toward him. 31 Meanwhile his disciples urged him, "Rabbi, eat something." 32 But he said to them, "I have food to eat that you know nothing about." 33 Then his disciples said to each other, "Could someone have brought him food?" 34 "My food," said Jesus, "is to do the will of him who sent me and to finish his work *The New International Version* (Grand Rapids, MI: Zondervan, 2011), Jn 4:27–34.

35 Don't you have a saying, 'It's still four months until harvest'? I tell you, open your eyes and look at the fields! They are ripe for harvest. 36 Even now the one who reaps draws a wage and harvests a crop for eternal life, so that the sower and the reaper may be glad

together. 37 Thus the saying 'One sows and another reaps' is true. 38 I sent you to reap what you have not worked for. Others have done the hard work, and you have reaped the benefits of their labor." *The New International Version* (Grand Rapids, MI: Zondervan, 2011), Jn 4:34–38.

39 Many of the Samaritans from that town believed in him because of the woman's testimony, "He told me everything I ever did." 40 So when the Samaritans came to him, they urged him to stay with them, and he stayed two days. 41 And because of his words many more became believers. *The New International Version* (Grand Rapids, MI: Zondervan, 2011), Jn 4:39–41.

Biblical Characters Who Are A Part Of Episode Of Episode 8

Jacob
Jacob is an actual biblical character found in several chapters of Genesis.
He did actually purchase land from the sons of Hamor. There is an actual Jacob's well mentioned in the Bible and Jesus did go to the well in John chapter four. The conversation between Jacob and the stranger, Hassib, is not found in the Scriptures.

The Woman At The Well
Although she is never named in the Scriptures, there is an actual woman at the well who comes to the well alone. She does have an actual conversation with

Jesus which is very close to the dialogue in the episode. Jesus does reveal himself to her as the Messiah, and she does go and tell others to come and see a man who told me everything I ever did. The Scriptures do not record the incidents with her in the marketplace or with her and her husband.

Matthew

Matthew is an actual biblical character who follows Jesus and hosts a party at his house for Jesus, the disciples and others. The party is viewed with disgust by the Pharisees. Much of the dialogue of Jesus between Jesus and the Pharisees is recorded in the Scriptures. The Scriptures do not mention the interruption by Gaius at the party.

Nicodemus

Nicodemus is mentioned three times in the gospel of John speaking favorably of Jesus. None of the appearances of Nicodemus found in this episode are actual biblical accounts recorded in the Scriptures.

The Disciples

The disciples that Jesus had called up until this point, did go with him to Samaria. They were not with Jesus when he spoke with the woman. The Scriptures do not record their disagreement with Jesus on the direction to go nor of the conflict spoken of by Jesus between the Jews and Samaritans.

Jesus

Jesus is an actual biblical character found throughout the New Testament books. Jesus does attend a party at Matthew's house and he does have a confrontation with the Pharisees over it. Jesus does actually go through Samaria and does meet with the woman at the well in chapter four of John's gospel. His dialogue with the woman at the well is very consistent with the biblical account found in chapter four of John.

Bible Study Discussion Questions Episode 8 "I AM He"

1. What did it take or what would it take to convince you that Jesus is the Messiah?

2. In the opening of the episode, Jacob makes the comment, they did not choose their God, but rather their God chose them. How are you encouraged by knowing that it was God who chose you?

3. What do you think life was like for the woman at the well before she encountered Jesus?

4. How did you feel about her husband as portrayed in the episode?

5. Have you ever been in a situation in which the other person seemed unreasonable in what you were asking them to do? How did you handle it?

6. What can we learn from Jesus' statement that God desires mercy more than sacrifice?

7. How can the strength of our independence keep us from getting closer to God?

8. Gaius wanted Matthew to turn away from following Jesus. Who has been a Gaius in your life seeking to turn you away from Christ?

9. What were your feelings about Nicodemus as he watched the disciples gather with Jesus as they prepared to leave Capernaum?

10. Why do you think Nicodemus left the bag of gold for them to find? How are we sometimes guilty of giving something instead of giving ourselves?

11.What do you think Jesus means when he offers us living water?

12.Why is the woman at the well so suspicious of Jesus?

13. Why do you think Jesus went out of his way to be present for this encounter with this Samaritan woman?

14.In the episode, Jesus has tears in his eyes as he concludes his talk with the woman at the well. What do you think moved Jesus the most about this woman?

15.Why does Jesus declare himself to be the Messiah to a Samaritan before he tells his own people?

,

16. Jesus breaks a tremendous barrier in this episode, but it's just the start. What barriers are we to be working on breaking down today?

17. What caused an evangelistic spirit in this woman that inspired her to want to go and tell others to come and see Jesus?

9 MEET THE AUTHOR

Rick Gillespie-Mobley has been a committed evangelical pastor since 1983. He currently is a part of A Covenant Order Of Evangelical Presbyterians (ECO). He is a gifted communicator and uses stories and humor in his messages in a way that engages his audiences. He has an extensive Christian background in several Christian denominations that include charismatics, Methodists, Church of God In Christ, Full Gospel, United Church Of Christ, Assemblies of God and Presbyterians.

Rick has a true love for the Scriptures as being the word of God and the authoritative interpretation for how we should live our lives today.

His background as a lawyer has given him a

unique way of analyzing the text in addition to the way he learned at seminary. He has put together this guide to help people to find the richness in the Chosen Series. If one is not aware of the Scriptures, some of the things in the series will just zip past you. Rick has gathered the Scriptures referred to in each episode along with a summary of each episode to assist people in watching the series. The group discussion questions are designed to allow for almost anyone to lead a discussion on the series.

Rick was married on August 30, 1980 to his bride Toby. They served together as co-pastors for nearly 38 years. In addition to their adult children Samantha, Anita (Milan), Keon (Ashley), and Sharon, they have served as foster parents for 20 years. Rick is a graduate of Hornell Senior High School in Hornell, NY, Hamilton College B.A. in Clinton, NY, Gordon Conwel Theological Seminary M. Div. in S. Hamilton, MA, Trinity Bible College & Seminary D. Min in Newburgh , IN and Boston University School of Law J.D in Boston, MA.

Rick has served with his wife Toby as co-pastors of Roxbury Presbyterian Church (6 years) in Boston, Ma, and Glenville New Life Community Church (24 years).

They also served as pastors in Cleveland, Oh at New Life Fellowship (4 Years) in Cleveland, OH, Calvary Presbyterian Church (2 years), and New Life At Calvary (8 years). Toby was honorably retired in 2020 and Rick was honorably retired in 2021.. Rick and Toby were both ordained in the Presbyterian Church of the United States Of America, but transferred their membership to A Covenant Order of Evangelical Presbyterian (ECO). Rick was admitted to practice law in both Massachusetts and Ohio.

Made in the USA
Las Vegas, NV
27 April 2023